Interactive Notebook: Physical Science

Authors: Schyrlet Cameron and Carolyn Craig

Editor: Mary Dieterich

Proofreaders: Cindy Neisen and Margaret Brown

COPYRIGHT © 2018 Mark Twain Media, Inc.

ISBN 978-1-62223-687-9

Printing No. CD-405010

Mark Twain Media, Inc., Publishers
Distributed by Carson-Dellosa Publishing LLC

Table of Contents

To the Teacher

The *Interactive Notebook* series consists of three books: *Physical Science, Life Science,* and *Earth and Space Science.* The series is designed to allow students to become active participants in their own learning by creating interactive science notebooks (ISN). Each book lays out an easy-to-follow plan for setting up, creating, and maintaining interactive notebooks for the science classroom.

An interactive science notebook is simply a spiral notebook that students use to store and organize important information. It is a culmination of student work throughout the unit of study. Once completed, the notebook becomes the student's own personalized science book and a great resource for reviewing and studying for tests.

The intent of the *Interactive Notebook* series is to help students make sense of new information. Textbooks often present more facts and data than students can process at one time. The books in this series introduce each science concept in an easy-to-read and easy-to-understand format that does not overwhelm the learner. The text presents only the most important information, making it easier for students to comprehend. Vocabulary words are printed in boldfaced type.

Interactive Notebook: Physical Science contains 29 lessons that cover three units of study: matter, forces and motion, and forms of energy. The units can be used in the order presented or in the order that best fits the science curriculum. Teachers can easily differentiate lessons to address the individual learning levels and needs of each student. The lessons are designed to support state and national standards. Each unit consists of two pages.

- **Input page:** essential information for a major science concept, instructions for a hands-on activity, and directions for extending learning
- **Output page:** hands-on activity such as a foldable or graphic organizer to help students process the unit

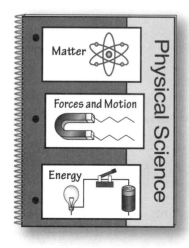

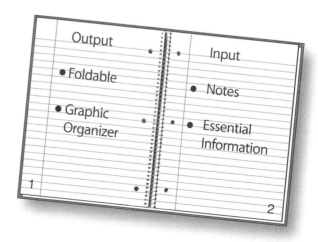

Organizing an Interactive Science Notebook (ISN)

What Is an Interactive Notebook?

Does this sound familiar? "I can't find my homework...class notes ...study guide." If so, the interactive science notebook (ISN) is a tool you can use to help manage this problem. An ISN is simply a notebook that students use to record, store, and organize their work. The "interactive" aspect of the notebook comes from the fact that students are working with information in various ways as they fill in the notebook. Once completed, the notebook becomes the student's own personalized study guide and a great resource for reviewing information, reinforcing concepts, and studying for tests.

Materials Needed to Create an ISN

- Notebook (spiral, composition, or binder with loose-leaf paper)
- Glue stick
- Scissors
- Colored pencils (we do not recommend using markers)
- Tabs

Creating an Interactive Science Notebook

A good time to introduce the interactive notebook is at the beginning of a new unit of study. Use the following steps to get started.

Step 1: *Notebook Cover*
Students design cover to reflect the three units of study (See pages 5 and 6). They should add their names and other important information as directed by the teacher.

Step 2: *Grading Rubric*
Take time to discuss the grading rubric with the students. It is important for each student to understand the expectations for creating the interactive notebook.

Step 3: *Table of Contents*
Students label the first several pages of the notebook "Table of Contents." When completing a new page, they then add its title to the table of contents.

Step 4: *Creating Pages*
The notebook is developed using the dual-page format. The right-hand side is the input page where essential information and notes from readings, videos, or observations, etc. are placed. The left-hand side is the output page reserved for folding activities, diagrams, graphic organizers, etc. Students number the front and back of each page in the bottom outside corner (odd: LEFT-side; even: RIGHT-side).

Step 5: *Tab Units*
Add a tab to the edge of the first page of each unit to make it easy to flip to the unit.

Step 6: *Glossary*
Reserve several pages at the back of the notebook where students can create a glossary of science terms. Students can add an entry for vocabulary words introduced in each unit.

Step 7: *Pocket*
Attach a pocket to the inside of the back cover of the notebook for storage of returned quizzes, class syllabus, and other items that don't seem to belong on pages of the notebook. This can be an envelope, resealable plastic bag, or students can design their own pocket.

Left-Hand and Right-Hand Notebook Pages

Interactive notebooks are usually viewed open like a textbook. This allows the student to view the left-hand page and right-hand page at the same time. You have several options for how to format the two pages. Traditionally, the right-hand page is used as the input or the content part of the lesson. The left-hand page is the student output part of the lesson. This is where the students have an opportunity to show what they have learned in a creative and colorful way. (Color helps the brain remember information better.) The lessons in this book use this format. However, you may prefer to switch the order so that the student output page is on the right and the input page is on the left.

Date: October 22
Standard: Develop model to describe the atomic structure.
Objective: identify parts of an atom.

Atom Diagram

Neutron
Electron
Nucleus
Proton

Reflection Statement
Atoms make up everything. That means I am made up of atoms.

1

Mini-Lesson
Everything is made of matter. **Matter** is made up of tiny particles called atoms. Each atom is made up of three even tinier particles. These particles are protons, electrons, and neutrons. The mass of each particle is measured in **amu** (atomic mass unit).

Vocabulary
Matter is made up of tiny particles called atoms
Amu is the unit for measuring atomic mass

2

Left-Hand Page   **Right-Hand Page**

The format of the interactive notebook involves both the right-brain and left-brain hemispheres to help students process information. When creating the pages, start with the left-hand page. First, have students date the page, then write the standards and learning objectives to be addressed in the lesson and the essential questions to be answered. Students then move to the right-hand page and the teacher-directed part of the lesson. Finally, students use the information they have learned to complete the left-hand page. The notebook below details different types of items and activities that could be included for each page.

Left-Hand Page
Student Output
(Odd-numbered pages)

- State Standard
- Learning Objectives
- Essential Questions
- Drawings
- Diagrams
- Illustrations
- Graphic Organizers
- Reflection Statements
- Summaries
- Conclusions
- Practice Problems
- Data from Experiments
- Charts and Graphs

1

Right-Hand Page
Input: Teacher-Directed/Content
(Even-numbered pages)

- Lecture Notes
- Textbook Notes
- Study Guides
- Video Notes
- Mini-Lessons
- Handouts
- Vocabulary
- Lab Notes
- Procedures for Experiments
- Example Problems
- Formulas
- Equations

2

Interactive Notebook Rubric

Directions: Review the grading rubric below. It lists the criteria that will be used to score your completed notebook. Place this page in your notebook.

Physical Science Interactive Notebook Grading Rubric

Category	Excellent (4)	Good Work (3)	Needs Improvement (2)	Incomplete (1)		
Organization	Table of contents and glossary completed. All notebook pages numbered, dated, and titled correctly.	Table of contents and glossary mostly completed. Most pages numbered, dated, and titled correctly.	Table of contents and glossary incomplete. Several pages not numbered, dated, or titled correctly.	Table of contents and/or glossary missing or incomplete. Little or no attempt to number, date, or title pages correctly.		
Content	All notebook pages completed. All information complete and accurate. All spelling correct.	Most notebook pages completed. One notebook page missing. Most information accurate. Most spelling correct.	Several missing or incomplete notebook pages. Most information inaccurate. Many spelling errors.	Many missing or incomplete notebook pages. Information inaccurate. Little or no attempt at correct spelling.		
Appearance	Notebook pages very neat and organized. Writing and graphics clear and colorful.	Most notebook pages neat and organized. Most writing and graphics clear and colorful.	Notebook pages messy and somewhat disorganized. Writing and graphics messy. Limited use of color to personalize work.	Notebook pages very messy and lack organization. Writing and graphics illegible.		

Student's Comments:

Teacher's Comments:

What Is Physical Science?

Mini-Lesson

Read the following information. Then cut out and attach this box to the right-hand page of your science notebook.

Physical science is one of several branches of science. It is the study of matter, force and motion, and energy. **Physicists** investigate such topics as atomic structure, chemical reactions, simple machines, gravity, and light.

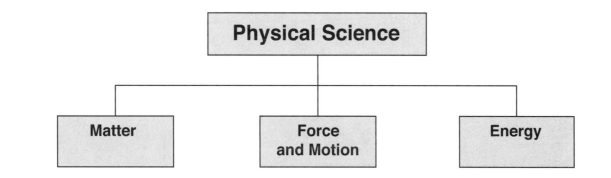

How to Create Your Physical Science Notebook Cover

Create a cover that will reflect your study of the three units you will explore in your study of physical science.

Step 1: Flip through your science textbook to get an idea of the content you will cover as you complete your study of physical science.

Step 2: Fill in the sections of the template with colorful drawings and diagrams.

Step 3: Cut out the template.

Step 4: Apply glue to the back of the template and attach to the front cover of your notebook.

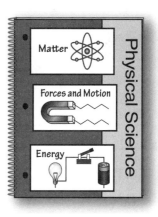

Reflect on What You Have Learned

Write a reflection statement on the left-hand page of your notebook.

Question: What have you learned about physical science that you did not know before this lesson? Support your answer with examples and details.

Physical Science Notebook Cover

Directions: Create a cover that will reflect your study of the three topics you will explore in your study of physical science. Fill in the sections of the template below with colorful drawings and diagrams. Cut out the template and glue to the front of your notebook.

Matter

Forces and Motion

Energy

Physical Science

First and Last Name: _____

Class Period: _____

Atomic Structure

Mini-Lesson

Read the following information. Then cut out and attach this box to the right-hand side of your science notebook. Use what you have learned to create the left-hand page for your notebook.

Everything is made of matter. **Matter** is made up of tiny particles called atoms. Each **atom** is made up of three even tinier particles. These particles are protons, electrons, and neutrons. The mass of each particle is measured in **amu** (atomic mass units).

Parts of an Atom

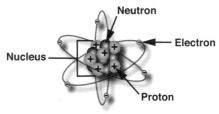

- The **nucleus** is the center of the atom. The protons and neutrons are located in the nucleus of the atom.
- The **protons** have a positive (+) electrical charge. The mass is approximately 1 amu.
- **Neutrons** are neutral and have no electrical charge. The mass is approximately 1 amu.
- **Electrons** are small particles in orbit around the nucleus in an area called the electron cloud. The electrons have a negative (-) electrical charge. They are organized into levels within the electron cloud, and the outermost level is referred to as the valence energy level. The mass of an electron is approximately 0.0018 amu.

How to Create Your Left-Hand Notebook Page

Complete the following steps to create the left-hand page of your physical science notebook. Use lots of color.

Step 1: Cut out the title and glue it to the top of the notebook page.

Step 2: Cut out the diagram box. Apply glue to the back of the gray tab and attach below title. Write the correct definition under the flap.

Step 3: Fill in the missing information in each box.

Step 4: Cut out and glue each box to the page.

Step 5: Draw a line from each box to the correct part of the diagram.

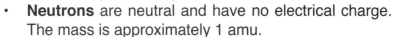

Demonstrate What You Have Learned

Create a three-dimensional model of an atom that can be hung from a string. Research one of the elements listed below. Use the information to draw a diagram of the atom. Make sure to display the correct number of neutrons, protons, and electrons; these should be in their correct locations. Gather the materials needed to construct your atom. Use the diagram to help build your model.

Elements: hydrogen   sodium   copper   carbon   calcium   gold

Atomic Structure

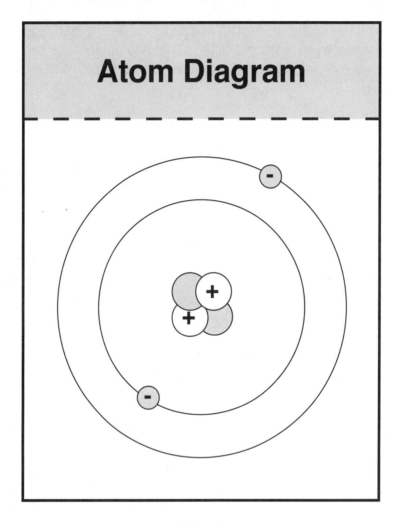

Atom Diagram

Proton	Neutron	Electron
Charge:	Charge:	Charge:
Mass:	Mass:	Mass:
Location:	Location:	Location:

8

Properties of Matter

Mini-Lesson

Read the following information. Then cut out and attach this box to the right-hand side of your science notebook. Use what you have learned to create the left-hand page for your notebook.

Matter is anything that has mass and volume. All matter has both physical and chemical properties. These **properties** are the characteristics or features that can help you identify or classify matter in its different forms, such as how it looks, feels, or acts.

- **Physical properties** are any of the characteristics of matter that can be observed or measured without changing the chemical structure of the substance. Some examples of physical properties are color, texture, density, volume, mass, boiling point, melting point, state, electrical conductivity, and solubility (ability to dissolve in other substances).
- **Chemical properties** are any of the characteristics of matter that describe its ability to change into a new substance. Some examples of chemical properties are oxidation (ability to combine with oxygen to burn, decay, or rust), reactivity (ability to combine chemically with other substances), and precipitation (ability to form a solid in a solution).

How to Create Your Left-Hand Notebook Page

Complete the following steps to create the left-hand page of your physical science notebook. Use lots of color.

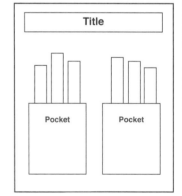

Step 1: Cut out the title and glue it to the top of the notebook page.

Step 2: Cut out the two pockets. Write the correct definition for each pocket. Fold back the gray tabs on the dotted lines. Apply glue to the tabs and attach the pockets to the page below the title.

Step 3: Cut out the vocabulary strips. Write a definition for each strip.

Step 4: Place each strip in the correct pocket.

Demonstrate What You Have Learned

Write a reflection statement on the left-hand page of your notebook.

Question: Based on what you have learned from the mini-lesson, is wind an example of matter or non-matter? Explain your answer.

Properties of Matter

Oxidation:	Density:
Texture:	Volume:
Solubility:	Reactivity:
Color:	Mass:
Boiling Point:	Electrical Conductivity:
Melting Point:	Precipitation:

Physical Properties

Definition: _____
_____
_____
_____
_____
_____
_____

Chemical Properties

Definition: _____
_____
_____
_____
_____
_____
_____

States of Matter

Mini-Lesson

Read the following information. Then cut out and attach this box to the right-hand side of your science notebook. Use what you have learned to create the left-hand page for your notebook.

Matter is made up of tiny particles called atoms and molecules. The arrangement of the particles determines the **state of the matter** or physical form. Each state is known as a **phase** of matter.

States of Matter

- **Solids** have a definite shape and volume. Solids keep their shape and do not conform to the shape of the container in which they are placed. Particles are packed tightly together in a fixed position. The particles vibrate, moving back and forth slightly.

- **Liquids** have a definite volume but no definite shape. Liquids will take the shape of the container in which they are placed. The particles move around freely, which allows a liquid to flow. For this reason, a liquid is also called a fluid.

- **Gases** have no definite volume or shape. A gas is a fluid. The gases will expand to fill any container and will take the shape of the container. Gas particles have a great deal of space between them and move all the time.

- **Plasma** has no definite shape or volume and is a highly energized gas consisting of nuclei and electrons. The particles are in constant motion. The gases will expand to fill any container and will take the shape of the container. Plasma is a fluid, like a liquid or gas.

How to Create Your Left-Hand Notebook Page

Complete the following steps to create the left-hand page of your physical science notebook. Use lots of color.

Step 1: Cut out the title and glue it to the top of the notebook page.

Step 2: Cut out the first chart. Apply glue to the back and attach below the title. Create a representation of the particles in each state of matter in the first row of boxes.

Step 3: Cut out the four illustrations and glue in the correct boxes in the second row on the chart.

Step 4: Cut out the second chart. Apply glue to the back and attach at the bottom of the page.

Step 5: For each phase of matter, check the box that describes a characteristic.

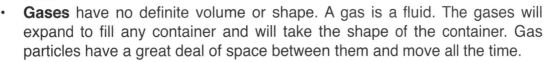
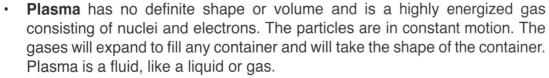

Demonstrate What You Have Learned

Construct a three-pocket folder by folding a horizontal sheet of paper into thirds. Fold the bottom edge up two inches and crease. Staple the two-inch tab to create three pockets. Label the pockets solid, liquid, and gas. Cut out examples of the three familiar forms of matter from magazines or print from the Internet. Store the pictures in the correct pocket.

States of Matter

Particles in Matter

Solid	Liquid	Gas	Plasma

Phases of Matter

Characteristics	Solid	Liquid	Gas	Plasma
Has a definite shape				
Has a definite volume				
Particles move freely				
Is a fluid				

Elements, Molecules, and Compounds

Mini-Lesson

Read the following information. Then cut out and attach this box to the right-hand side of your science notebook. Use what you have learned to create the left-hand page for your notebook.

    Matter is anything that has mass and takes up space. Matter is made up of tiny particles called atoms. An **atom** is the smallest part of an element.

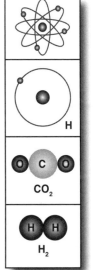

- An **element** is a pure substance made of only one kind of atom. An element cannot be broken down into simpler substances. Carbon, oxygen, hydrogen, and nitrogen are elements. Elements are listed and classified on the Periodic Table.
- A **compound** is a substance that is made up of two or more different atoms chemically joined together. For example, carbon dioxide (CO_2) is a compound.
- A **molecule** is the smallest part of a compound. A molecule is two or more atoms that are chemically bonded. For example, a hydrogen molecule (H_2) is made up of two hydrogen atoms. Most molecules are made up of two or more atoms of different elements. For example, a water molecule (H_2O) is made up of two hydrogen (H) atoms and one oxygen (O) atom.

How to Create Your Left-Hand Notebook Page

Complete the following steps to create the left-hand page of your physical science notebook. Use lots of color.

Title		
Type of Matter	Definiton	Diagram

How Many?

Step 1: Cut out the title and glue it to the top of the notebook page.
Step 2: Cut out the chart. Apply glue to the back and attach below the title.
Step 3: Cut apart the eight picture and definition cards and glue in the correct box on the chart.
Step 4: Cut out the How Many? box and fill in the blanks. Glue the box at the bottom of page beneath the chart.

Demonstrate What You Have Learned

    Construct a water molecule and a carbon dioxide molecule using a variety of colored mini-marshmallows and toothpicks. If you need help, use an online source or your science textbook.

Elements, Molecules, and Compounds

Type of Matter	Definition	Diagram
Atom		
Element		
Compound		
Molecule		

How Many?

NO$_2$
nitrogen dioxide

Atoms _____

Elements _____

Molecules _____

Compounds _____

a substance that is made up of two or more different atoms chemically joined together	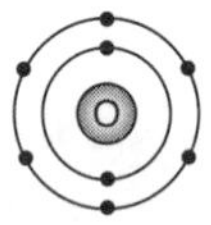
smallest part of an element	
a pure substance made of only one kind of atom	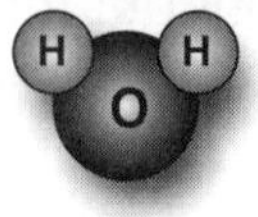
two or more atoms chemically joined together	

Chemical Bonds

Mini-Lesson

Read the following information. Then cut out and attach this box to the right-hand side of your science notebook. Use what you have learned to create the left-hand page for your notebook.

The elements in a compound are held together by chemical bonds. A **chemical bond** is the force of attraction between the atoms of the elements in a compound. Chemical bonds occur when atoms either transfer or share electrons. There are two main types of chemical bonds.

An **ionic bond** is formed when atoms transfer electrons. **Ionic compounds** are compounds formed with ionic bonds. Table salt is an example of an ionic compound.

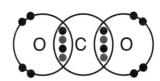

Na   Cl
Sodium chloride

A **covalent bond** is formed when atoms share electrons. **Covalent compounds** are compounds formed with covalent bonds. Water and carbon dioxide are examples of a covalent compound.

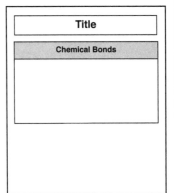

Carbon dioxide

How to Create Your Left-Hand Notebook Page

Complete the following steps to create the left-hand page of your physical science notebook. Use lots of color.

Step 1: Cut out the title and glue it to the top of the notebook page.

Step 2: Cut out the chart. Apply glue to the back and attach below the title.

Step 3: Cut out the picture and word cards. Glue in the correct box on the chart.

Title
Chemical Bonds

Demonstrate What You Have Learned

Make a list of five compounds with ionic bonds and five compounds with covalent bonds. Use an online source or your textbook if you need help.

Chemical Bonds

Chemical Bond	Definition	Example

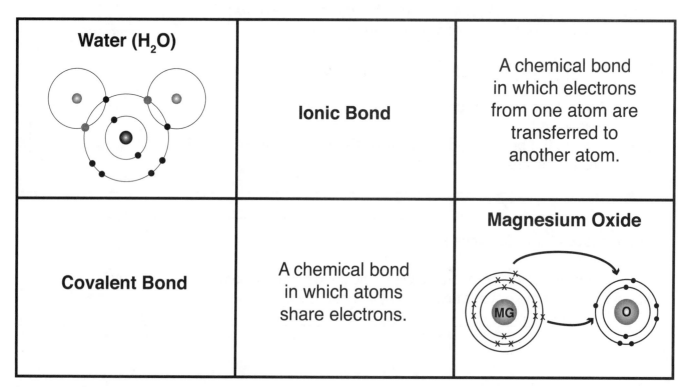

Water (H_2O)	Ionic Bond	A chemical bond in which electrons from one atom are transferred to another atom.
Covalent Bond	A chemical bond in which atoms share electrons.	Magnesium Oxide

Periodic Table of Elements

Mini-Lesson

Read the following information. Then cut out and attach this box to the right-hand side of your science notebook. Use what you have learned to create the left-hand page for your notebook.

The **Periodic Table of Elements** is a chart where all the known elements are organized according to their properties. Each column of elements is called a **group** or **family**. Elements in the same group have similar chemical properties. They usually react the same in chemical reactions, look the same, and can be used for the same purposes. Each row is called a **period**. There are seven periods on the periodic table. The lanthanides and actinides are usually written at the bottom of the table for convenience, but they really fit in with the sixth and seventh periods.

By studying the Periodic Table, you can quickly discover a lot about an element. Many tables include keys to help you identify elements as metals, nonmetals, or metalloids. Some Periodic Tables even tell us whether an element is a solid, liquid, or gas at room temperature or if an element occurs somewhere in nature or is manmade (synthetic).

Each box on the Periodic Table represents an element and displays specific information about the element. Different Periodic Tables include different information. An example is shown at the right.

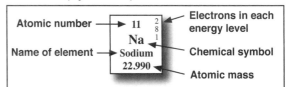

How to Create Your Left-Hand Notebook Page

Complete the following steps to create the left-hand page of your physical science notebook.

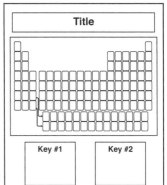

Step 1: Cut out the title and glue it to the top of the notebook page.

Step 2: Cut out the Periodic Table. Apply glue to the back and attach below the title.

Step 3: Choose the colors for the boxes in Key #1 and color them in. Cut out Key #1 and Key #2. Apply glue to the back and attach below the Periodic Table.

Step 4: Identify elements that can be classified as metals, nonmetals, or metalloids. Refer to your science textbook for help. Color code the element boxes on the Periodic Table to correspond to Key #1.

Step 5: Draw the correct symbol from Key #2 in the upper right-hand corner of each element box it correctly identifies. Refer to your science textbook for help.

Demonstrate What You Have Learned

Create a cube for one of the elements on the Periodic Table. On one face of the cube, copy the information from the Periodic Table about the element you have selected. Research your element and write sentences on the other faces about the element's appearance, properties, and uses.

Periodic Table of Elements

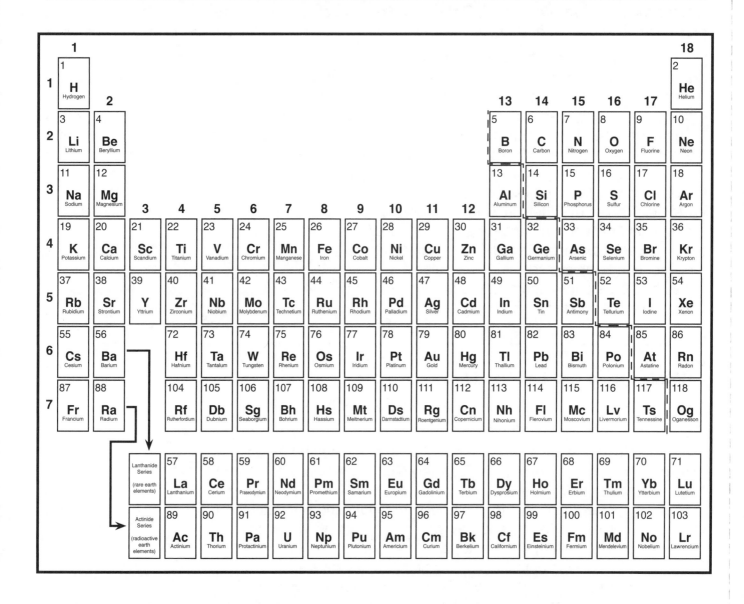

Key #1

- ☐ **Metal**
- ☐ **Metalloid**
- ☐ **Nonmetal**

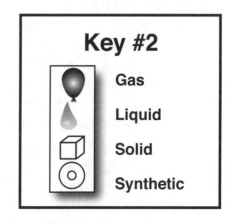

Key #2

- **Gas**
- **Liquid**
- **Solid**
- **Synthetic**

Mixtures

Mini-Lesson

Read the following information. Then cut out and attach this box to the right-hand side of your science notebook. Use what you have learned to create the left-hand page for your notebook.

A **mixture** is a substance made by combining two or more different substances without a chemical reaction occurring. The substances in the mixture keep their properties and can be separated by physical means. For example, a fruit salad is a mixture.

There are two main categories of mixtures: homogeneous mixtures and heterogeneous mixtures. In a **homogenous** mixture, all the substances are evenly distributed throughout the mixture (air). In a **heterogeneous** mixture, the substances are not evenly distributed (chocolate chip cookies).

Kinds of Mixtures

- A **solution** is a mixture that looks like a single substance and has the same properties throughout. Salt water is a mixture that is a solution. A solution can be made up of different combinations of solids, liquids, and gases. A cola drink is an example of a solution made up of a liquid and a gas. A solution has two parts: a solute and a solvent. For example, salt water is a solution. Salt (the substance that dissolves) is the **solute.** Water (the substance in which the salt dissolves) is the **solvent**.
- A **suspension** is a mixture in which the particles are dispersed but are large enough to see and to settle out. For example, hot chocolate is a mixture that is a suspension. The cocoa particles will settle to the bottom of the cup.
- A **colloid** is a mixture in which the small, undissolved particles do not settle out. Milk is an example of a colloid. Fats and proteins in the milk form globular particles that are too small to be seen and do not settle out.

How to Create Your Left-Hand Notebook Page

Complete the following steps to create the left-hand page of your physical science notebook. Use lots of color.

Step 1: Cut out the title and glue it to the top of the page.

Step 2: Cut out the graphic organizer chart. Apply glue to the back and attach below the title.

Step 3: Cut out the word cards and glue one on each arrow.

Step 4: Cut out the 3 picture flaps. Apply glue to the back of each gray tab. Glue each flap in the correct box below the word cards.

Step 5: Write the correct definition under each flap.

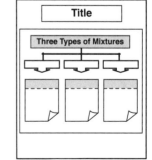

Demonstrate What You Have Learned

Add 200 mL of hot water to two beakers. Add a heaped teaspoon of sugar to one beaker. Add the same amount of cocoa or chocolate drinking powder to the other. Stir each briefly for the same length of time. Explain what happened using terms you learned from the lesson.

Mixtures

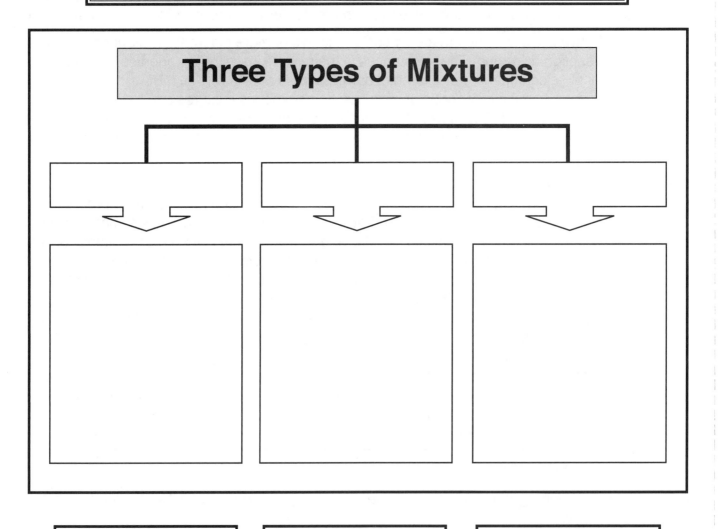

Three Types of Mixtures

Colloid	Solution	Suspension

Salt Water	Glass of Milk	Cup of Hot Cocoa

pH – Acids and Bases

Mini-Lesson

Read the following information. Then cut out and attach this box to the right-hand side of your science notebook. Use what you have learned to create the left-hand page for your notebook.

An **acid** is a chemical compound that has a pH below 7.0, a sour taste, and releases hydroxyl ions in water. Some foods contain acid, such as lemon juice. Many acids are too strong to taste or even touch. One of the strongest acids is sulfuric acid (battery acid).

Chemical compounds that taste bitter, feel slippery, dissolve oils and fats, and conduct electricity are called **bases** (alkaline). Ammonia, lye, and bleach are bases. Like acids, strong bases can also be dangerous to taste or touch.

Sometimes the substance we are testing is neither an acid nor a base. It is a **neutral** substance. When an acid and a base react chemically, they neutralize each other. Water is a neutral substance. Salt is another neutral compound produced when acids and bases react chemically.

A **pH scale** is a tool for measuring acids and bases. The scale ranges from 0–14. **Litmus paper** is an indicator used to tell if a substance is an acid or a base. The color of the paper matches up with the numbers on the pH scale

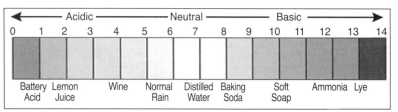

pH Scale

to indicate what kind of substance is being tested. (Acids turn blue litmus paper red. Bases turn red litmus paper blue). A substance with a pH of 7 is classified as a neutral (neither acid nor base). A substance with a pH below 7 is classified as an acid. A substance with a pH above 7 is classified as a base.

How to Create Your Left-Hand Notebook Page

Complete the following steps to create the left-hand page of your physical science notebook. Use lots of color.

Step 1: Cut out the title and glue it to the top of the page.

Step 2: Cut out the chart. Apply glue to the back and attach below the title.

Step 3: Write the correct definition in each box on the chart.

Step 4: Cut out the picture cards. Apply glue to the back of each card and glue in the correct example box on the chart.

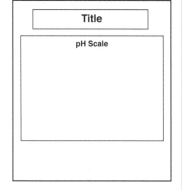

Demonstrate What You Have Learned

You learned litmus paper is an indicator used to tell if a substance is an acid or a base. Use litmus paper to test various substances such as lemon juice, ammonia, cleaning products, tap water, pure water, and soft drinks to determine if they are acidic, neutral, or basic (alkaline).

pH – Acids and Bases

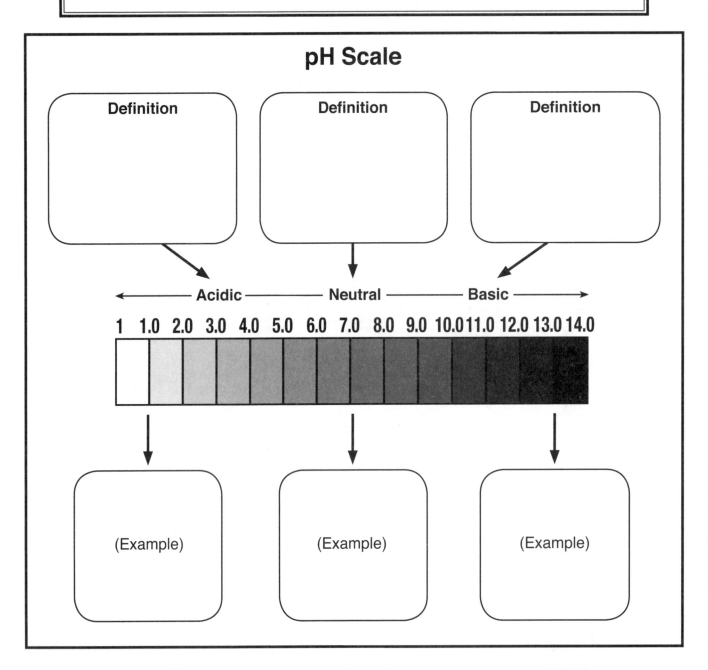

pH Scale

Definition

Definition

Definition

←———— Acidic ————— Neutral ————— Basic ————→

1 1.0 2.0 3.0 4.0 5.0 6.0 7.0 8.0 9.0 10.0 11.0 12.0 13.0 14.0

(Example)

(Example)

(Example)

Lye

Glass of Water

Battery Acid

Mass vs. Weight

Mini-Lesson

Read the following information. Then cut out and attach this box to the right-hand side of your science notebook. Use what you have learned to create the left-hand page for your notebook.

Gravity is a force that attracts one object to another. You do not notice the pull of gravity. The force of gravity can be measured.

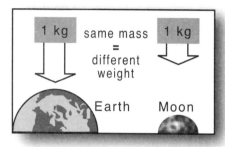

Weight is the measurement of the pull of gravity on an object. When you step on a bathroom scale, the scale shows your weight. The scale tells you that gravity is pulling on you. It is pulling you toward the center of the earth. It is the force of gravity that causes your weight to show on the scale. Scientists measure weight in newtons (N). Weight changes depending on the location of the object in the universe.

Mass is a measurement of the amount of matter (stuff) in an object. A balance is used to measure mass in kilograms (kg) and grams (g) by comparing a known amount of matter to an unknown amount of matter. The mass of an object always stays the same and doesn't change when an object moves from place to place. To understand mass, think of two balls. They are the same size. However, one is made of iron. The other is a hollow plastic ball. The iron ball weighs more. It has more mass. The amount of mass in an object is always the same regardless of where it is in the universe.

How to Create Your Left-Hand Notebook Page

Complete the following steps to create the left-hand page of your physical science notebook. Use lots of color.

Step 1: Cut out the title and glue it to the top of the page.
Step 2: Cut out the flap chart. Apply glue to the back of the gray tab and attach below the title. Write the correct definition under the flap.
Step 3: Cut out the second chart. Apply glue to the back and attach at the bottom of the page.
Step 4: Cut out the picture and word cards. Glue each card in the correct box on the chart.

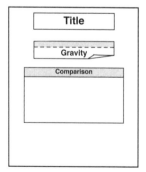

Demonstrate What You Have Learned

Estimate the weight and mass of four objects. Use a scale and balance to check your estimates. How close to the actual values were your estimates?

Mass vs. Weight

Gravity

Comparison			
Category	Definition	Measuring Tool	SI Unit
Mass			
Weight			

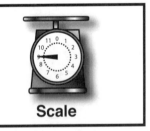

Scale

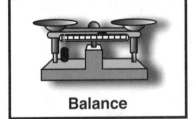

Balance

the amount of
gravitational
force acting
on an object

newtons (N)

the amount of
matter in an
object

kilograms (kg)
and grams (g)

Friction

Mini-Lesson

Read the following information. Then cut out and attach this box to the right-hand side of your science notebook. Use what you have learned to create the left-hand page for your notebook.

Friction is a resistance to motion. It is a force that can be used to slow down and stop moving objects. A driver applying the brakes to stop a car is an example. Friction is created whenever objects rub against each other, such as rubbing your hands together. Friction can produce heat and wear objects down. A way to reduce friction is to use a lubricant like grease or oil. Machines use lubricants to reduce friction and wear so they can last longer.

Four Types of Friction

- **Static friction** is the resistance that occurs when an object rests on a surface such as the tires of a car resting on pavement.
- **Sliding friction** is resistance that occurs when an object slides over a surface. Examples include sliding a piece of furniture over the floor or writing with a pencil.
- **Rolling friction** is resistance that occurs when an object rolls over a surface. Several examples include bicycles, cars, 4-wheelers, roller skates, skateboards, and ball bearings.
- **Fluid friction** is resistance that occurs when an object moves through a fluid. Fluids include liquids and gasses. For example, fluid friction is the resistance of air against an airplane or water against a swimmer's body.

How to Create Your Left-Hand Notebook Page

Complete the following steps to create the left-hand page of your physical science notebook. Use lots of color.

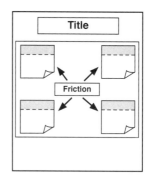

Step 1: Cut out the title and glue it to the top of the page.
Step 2: Cut out the graphic organizer chart. Apply glue to the back and attach below the title.
Step 3: Write a definition for friction.
Step 4: Cut out the picture flaps. Apply glue to the back of each gray tab and glue one in each box. Write the correct definition under each flap.

Demonstrate What You Have Learned

Observe what happens when a lubricant is used to reduce friction. Rub the palms of your hands together quickly for 30 seconds. Think about how it felt. Put a few drops of liquid dish soap on your hands. Rub your hands together quickly for 30 seconds. Observe what happens when a lubricant is used to reduce the friction between your hands.

Friction

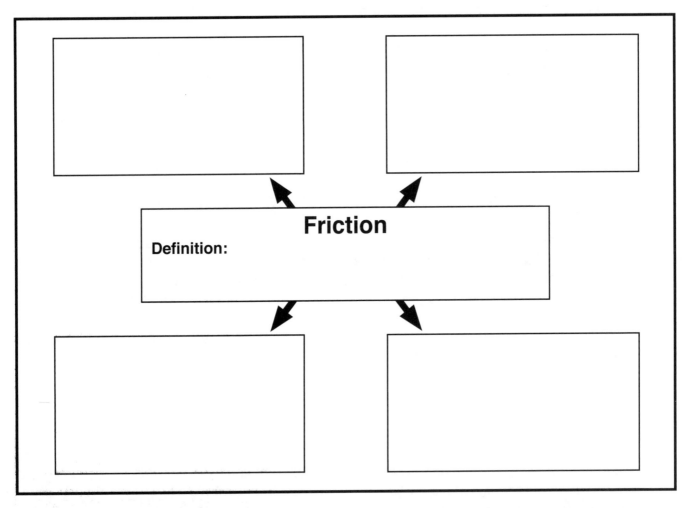

Friction

Definition:

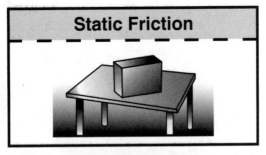

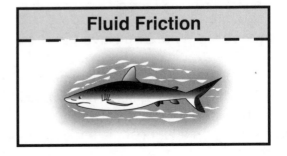

Newton's Laws of Motion

Mini-Lesson

Read the following information. Then cut out and attach this box to the right-hand side of your science notebook. Use what you have learned to create the left-hand page for your notebook.

Motion is the act of moving from one place to another. **Newton's Laws of Motion** explain the relationship between force and motion. Isaac Newton was the English scientist who stated the three laws of motion in 1687. The laws were named after him.

- The **First Law (Law of Inertia)** states an object at rest stays at rest until acted upon by another force; it stays in motion in a straight line at a constant speed until acted upon by another force. If a ball is not moving, it will stay that way until some force makes it move. **Inertia** is the tendency of objects to resist a change in their state of motion.

- The **Second Law (Law of Acceleration)** states that acceleration produced by a force on a body is directly proportional to the magnitude of the net force, is in the same direction as the force, and is inversely proportional to the mass of the body. For example, if two bike riders pedal with the same force, the rider moving less mass accelerates faster. **Acceleration** is the rate of change in the velocity of an object. **Velocity** is speed in a given direction.

- The **Third Law (Law of Action and Reaction)** states that for every action there is an equal and opposite reaction. For example, a boy jumps on a trampoline. The **action force** is the boy pushing down on the trampoline. The **reaction force** is the trampoline pushing up on the boy.

How to Create Your Left-Hand Notebook Page

Complete the following steps to create the left-hand page of your physical science notebook. Use lots of color.

Step 1: Cut out the title and glue it to the top of the page.
Step 2: Cut out the flap chart. Cut on the solid lines to create six flaps. Apply glue to the back of the gray center section of the chart only and attach it below the title.
Step 3: Write the correct definition under each flap.

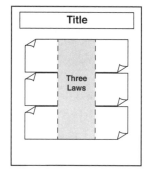

Demonstrate What You Have Learned

Observe Newton's Third Law of Motion in action. With a partner, thread fishing line through a straw. Attach one end of the fishing line to a table. Blow up a long balloon, then pinch off the opening, keeping air from escaping. Tape the straw to the balloon, still holding the balloon closed. Next, hold the fishing line taut and release the balloon. Which action do you think was the action force and which was the reaction force?

Newton's Laws of Motion

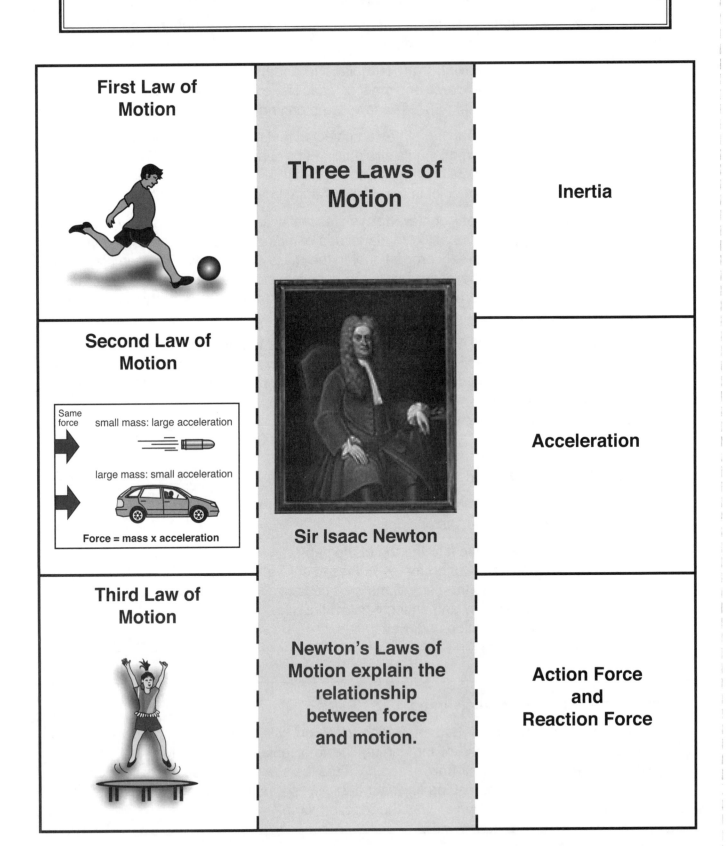

First Law of Motion

Three Laws of Motion

Inertia

Second Law of Motion

Same force

small mass: large acceleration

large mass: small acceleration

Force = mass x acceleration

Sir Isaac Newton

Acceleration

Third Law of Motion

Newton's Laws of Motion explain the relationship between force and motion.

Action Force and Reaction Force

Work

Mini-Lesson

Read the following information. Then cut out and attach this box to the right-hand side of your science notebook. Use what you have learned to create the left-hand page for your notebook.

Work in everyday language has many meanings. In physical science, **work** is the force needed to move an object through a distance. Pushing, pulling, and lifting are common forms of work. Work is done when a force acts on a body and moves it. You do work when you raise a 20-kilogram load to your shoulder or when you carry the load up a flight of stairs or push it across the floor.

Two factors must be considered when measuring work: (1) the force applied and (2) the distance through which the force acts. In work, distance is the change of position of an object. Work is measured in newtons-per-meter, which is called **joules** (J).

Calculating Work: **W = F x d** (W = work, F = force, and d= distance).

Problem: A student pushes a large box with a force of 20 newtons over a distance of 5 meters. How much work was done?

Solution:
W = F x d
W = 20 newtons x 5 meters
W = 100 joules

How to Create Your Left-Hand Notebook Page

Complete the following steps to create the left-hand page of your physical science notebook. Use lots of color.

Step 1: Cut out the title and glue it to the top of the page.

Step 2: Cut out the flap chart. Cut on the solid lines to create two flaps. Apply glue to the back of the top of the chart and attach it below the title.

Step 3: Write the correct definition under the first flap.

Step 4: Solve the problem for how much work is being done in the picture and write the answer under the second flap. Label your answer in joules.

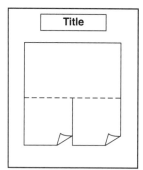

Title

Demonstrate What You Have Learned

Work with a partner. Write a word problem that requires calculating the work being done by a force. Trade and solve problems.

Work

How Much Work Is Being Done?

100 newtons
force

3 meters
distance

| Work | W = F x d |

Forces in Fluids

Mini-Lesson

Read the following information. Then cut out and attach this box to the right-hand side of your science notebook. Use what you have learned to create the left-hand page for your notebook.

Physical scientists describe **fluids** as any material that has no definite shape and has the ability to flow. Liquid, gas, and plasma are fluids. The molecules that make up these fluids do exert a pressure on surfaces with which they come in contact. Fluids move from an area of high pressure to one of low pressure.

Archimedes' principle states that a body immersed in fluid experiences a buoyant force equal to the weight of the fluid it displaces. For example, a lump of steel will sink because it is unable to **displace** (push aside) water that equals its weight. However, steel of the same weight shaped as a bowl will float. This is because the weight gets distributed over a larger area, and the steel displaces an amount of water equal to its weight. A ship floats because its total weight is exactly equal to the weight of the water it displaces.

Bernoulli's principle states that in fluid flow, an increase in **velocity** (speed) causes a decrease in **pressure** (force). This means the faster a fluid flows, the less pressure it exerts. An aircraft can achieve **lift** (upward force) because of the shape of its wings. They are shaped so that air flows faster over the top of the wing and slower underneath. Fast-moving air equals low air pressure while slow-moving air equals high air pressure. The high pressure underneath the wings will, therefore, push the aircraft up through the lower air pressure.

Pascal's principle states that a change in the pressure applied to an enclosed container is transmitted without change throughout the fluid and acts in all directions. Pascal worked in the field of **hydrodynamics**, which deals with the power of moving fluids. An example is a tire pump. When you pump a bike tire, you apply force on the pump that in turn exerts a force on the air inside the tire. The air responds by pushing not only on the pump but also against the walls of the tire. As a result, the pressure increases by an equal amount throughout the tire.

How to Create Your Left-Hand Notebook Page

Complete the following steps to create the left-hand page of your physical science notebook. Use lots of color.

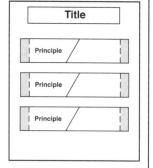

Step 1: Cut out the title and glue it to the top of the page.

Step 2: Cut out the six flaps. Pair the word flap with the correct picture flap. Apply glue to the back of each gray tab and attach below the title. Make sure the paired flaps meet in the middle.

Step 3: Write the correct definition under each flap pair.

Demonstrate What You Have Learned

Find the volume of an irregular object, such as a rock, by using a method called displacement. Add water to a graduated cylinder and record the volume. Add the rock and record the volume again. The difference between the first measurement and the second is the volume of the rock.

Forces in Fluids

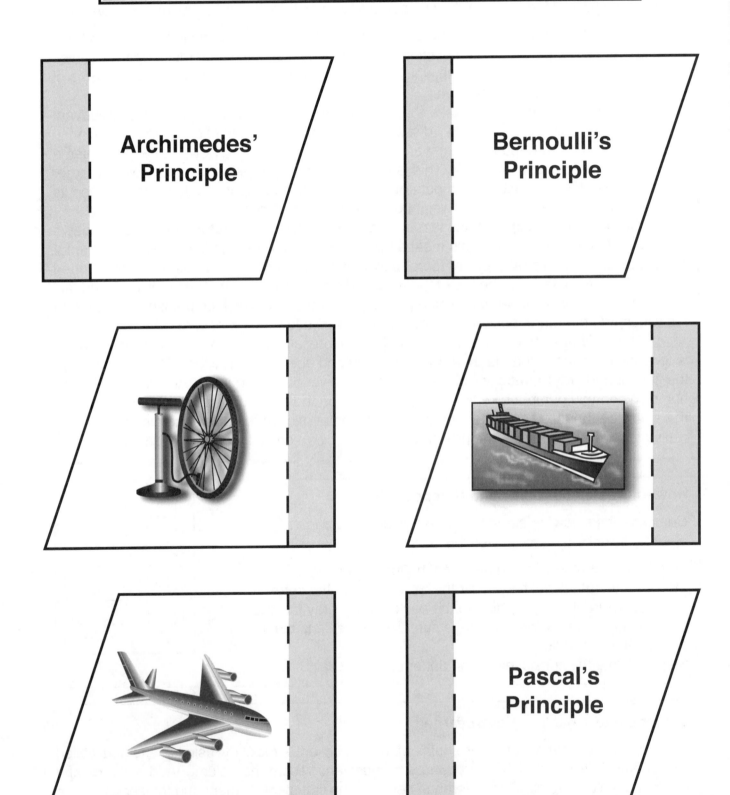

Archimedes'
Principle

Bernoulli's
Principle

Pascal's
Principle

Simple Machines

Mini-Lesson

Read the following information. Then cut out and attach this box to the right-hand side of your science notebook. Use what you have learned to create the left-hand page for your notebook.

Machines have changed the way in which we do work. A **machine** is any device that makes doing work easier. They reduce the force you have to apply to do the work. There are advantages of using a machine: (1) makes doing work easier by reducing the force exerted, (2) changes the distance over which the force is exerted, and (3) changes the direction of the force.

Some of the machines we use every day are **simple machines**. They have few or no moving parts to them. These machines help us to move objects closer, apart, or to raise them to different levels by increasing the force or changing the direction of the force.

Simple machines are designed to do specific jobs.
- A **lever** is a rigid bar that is free to rotate about a point called a fulcrum.
- The **pulley** is a wheel that turns readily on an axle. The axle is usually mounted on a frame.
- The **wheel and axle** is a wheel rigidly fixed to an axle.
- The **inclined plane** is a device that allows us to increase the height of an object without lifting it vertically.
- The **wedge** is a double inclined plane.
- The **screw** is an inclined plane wound around a cylinder.

How to Create Your Left-Hand Notebook Page

Complete the following steps to create the left-hand page of your physical science notebook. Use lots of color.

Step 1: Cut out the title and glue it to the top of the page.

Step 2: Cut out the flap chart. Cut on the solid lines to create six flaps. Apply glue to the back of the gray center section of the chart only and attach below the title.

Step 3: Cut apart the word cards. Glue each card in the correct box on the flap chart.

Step 4: Write the correct definition under each flap.

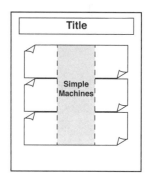

Demonstrate What You Have Learned

Most of the work the human body does involves simple machines. What type of simple machine do you think your teeth resemble when you bite into an apple? What type of simple machine do you think your arm resembles when it bends at the elbow to lift a heavy bucket of water?

Simple Machines

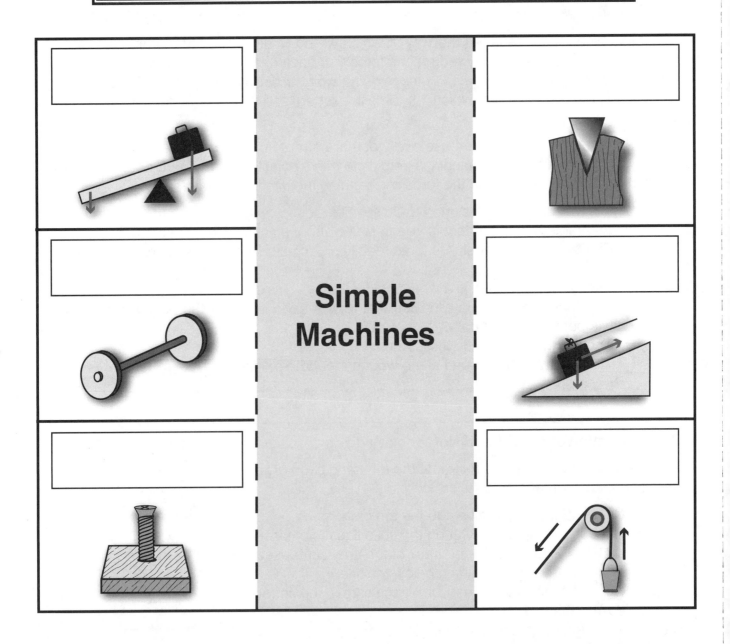

Simple Machines

Lever	Pulley	Wheel and Axle
Inclined Plane	Wedge	Screw

Forms of Energy

Mini-Lesson

Read the following information. Then cut out and attach this box to the right-hand side of your science notebook. Use what you have learned to create the left-hand page for your notebook.

Energy is a property of matter; it comes in many different forms. Energy cannot be created or destroyed; it can only change form. This rule is known as the Law of Conservation of Energy.

Forms of Energy
- **Mechanical energy** is the energy an object has because of its motion or position. There are two kinds of mechanical energy—kinetic and potential. **Kinetic energy** is the energy an object has because it is moving. **Potential energy** is stored energy.
- **Thermal energy** is the energy related to the temperature of a substance.
- **Light energy** is the energy carried by light and other kinds of electromagnetic waves.
- **Sound energy** is the energy carried by sound waves.
- **Electrical energy** is the energy produced by electrical charges.
- **Chemical energy** is the energy stored in chemical bonds.
- **Nuclear energy** is the energy contained in the nuclei of atoms.

How to Create Your Left-Hand Notebook Page

Complete the following steps to create the left-hand page of your physical science notebook. Use lots of color.

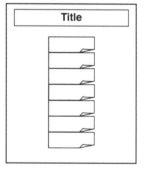

Step 1: Cut out the title and glue it to the top of the notebook page.
Step 2: Cut out the foldable chart.
Step 3: Fold the chart in half along the dotted line.
Step 4: Unfold and cut on the solid lines to create seven flaps.
Step 5: Apply glue to the back of the chart and attach below the title.
Step 6: Write the correct definition for each form of energy under each flap.

Demonstrate What You Have Learned

Fold a sheet of paper in half along the short side. Create two flaps by making one cut in the center of one side up to the fold line. Label the top of the two flaps, one "Kinetic Energy," the other "Potential Energy." Draw an example of each form of energy under the correct flap.

Forms of Energy

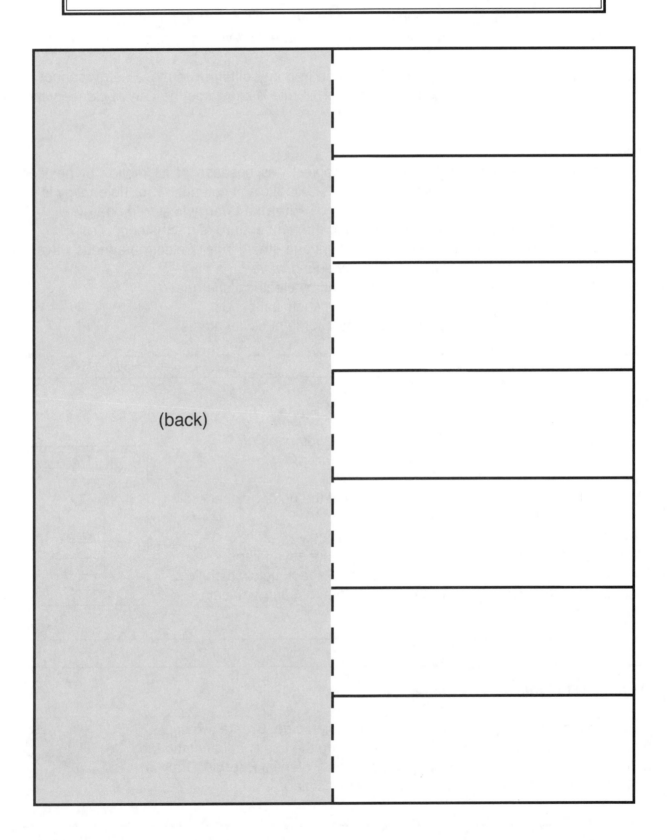

(back)

Methods of Heat Transfer

Mini-Lesson

Read the following information. Then cut out and attach this box to the right-hand side of your science notebook. Use what you have learned to create the left-hand page for your notebook.

Heat is thermal energy that is transferred from one object to another when the objects are different temperatures. Heat always flows from a warmer to a cooler object. When two substances come into contact, their particles collide. The energy from the faster-moving particles is transferred to the slower-moving particles, until the particles in both substances are moving at the same speed and their temperature has equalized. The three methods of heat transfer are conduction, convection, and radiation.

Methods of Heat Transfer

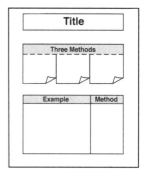

- **Conduction** is the transfer of heat from a warmer substance to a cooler substance through direct contact.
- **Convection** is the transfer of heat by the movement of fluids (like water and air) through currents.
- **Radiation** is the transfer of energy as electromagnetic waves. Electromagnetic waves can transmit heat through a vacuum or empty space. This energy comes in different wavelengths: radio, microwaves, infrared, visible light, ultraviolet light, x-rays, and gamma rays.

How to Create Your Left-Hand Notebook Page

Complete the following steps to create the left-hand page of your physical science notebook. Use lots of color.

Step 1: Cut out the title and glue it to the top of the notebook page.

Step 2: Cut out the flap chart. Cut on the solid lines to create three flaps. Apply glue to the back of the gray tab and attach below the title.

Step 3: Cut out the three picture cards and glue on the correct flap. Write the correct definition under each flap.

Step 4: Complete the second chart. Cut it out and glue at the bottom of the page.

Title
Three Methods

Example	Method

Demonstrate What You Have Learned

Write a reflection statement on the left-hand page of your notebook.

<u>Question</u>: What do you think would happen if we could only use one type of heat? Explain your answer.

Methods of Heat Transfer

Three Methods		
Conduction	**Convection**	**Radiation**

Example	Method of Transfer
1. rattlesnake uses infrared sensors to find prey in the dark	
2. hot air balloon rising into the air	
3. a pan from the oven is hot to the touch	
4. sun heating the earth	
5. spoon becomes warm in a cup of hot soup	
6. heating a pot of water on the stove	
7. drying wet boots over a floor vent	
8. getting a tan on the beach	
9. ice cubes melting in your hand	

Characteristics of Waves

Mini-Lesson

Read the following information. Then cut out and attach this box to the right-hand side of your science notebook. Use what you have learned to create the left-hand page for your notebook.

One way energy is transported is through waves. A **wave** is the direction and speed energy travels in a back-and-forth or up-and-down motion. The highest point of a wave is called the **crest**. The lowest point is called the **trough**. The **height** of a wave is the distance from its crest to its trough. The length of a wave is the distance from its crest to the crest of the next wave. One-half the distance from the crest to the trough is the wave's **amplitude**.

Mechanical and electromagnetic waves are the two main types of waves. **Mechanical waves** are waves that can travel through matter. **Electromagnetic waves** are waves that can travel through empty space.

Four Characteristics of Waves
- **Amplitude** is the distance a wave moves from its resting position. The larger the amplitude, the more energy carried by the wave.
- **Wavelength** is the distance from any point on one wave to a corresponding point on an adjacent wave.
- **Frequency** is the number of wavelengths that pass a given point in one second. Frequency is measured in hertz (Hz); one hertz is equal to one wave per second.
- **Wave speed** is the distance a wave travels divided by the time it takes to travel that distance. Waves move faster through some mediums than through others.

How to Create Your Left-Hand Notebook Page

Complete the following steps to create the left-hand page of your physical science notebook. Use lots of color.

Step 1: Cut out the title and glue it to the top of the notebook page.

Step 2: Cut out the flap chart. Cut on the solid line to create two vocabulary flaps. Apply glue to the back of the gray tab and attach below the title. Write the correct definition under each flap.

Step 3: Cut out the diagram box. Apply glue to the back and attach below the vocabulary flap chart.

Step 4: Cut out the word cards and glue in the correct box on the diagram.

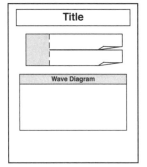

Demonstrate What You Have Learned

Shake a rope attached to a doorknob, causing a wave motion. The rope moves up and down, creating high points and low points.

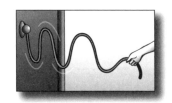

Characteristics of Waves

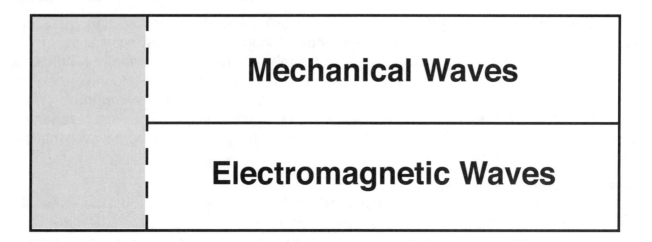

Mechanical Waves

Electromagnetic Waves

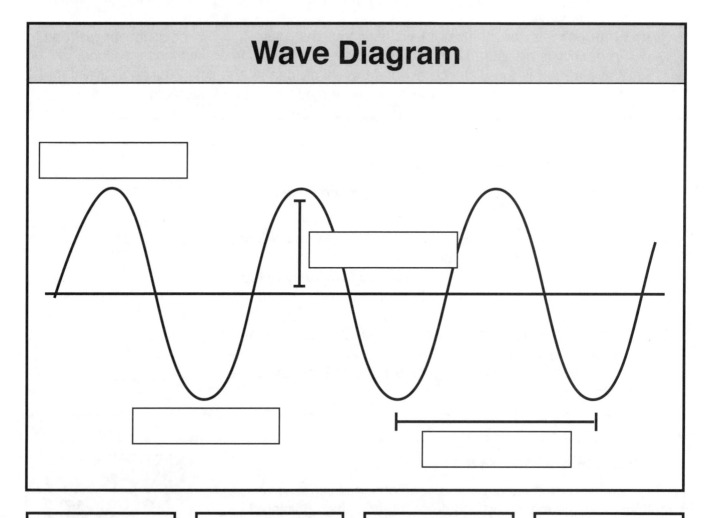

| Trough | Amplitude | Wavelength | Crest |

Kinds of Waves

Mini-Lesson

Read the following information. Then cut out and attach this box to the right-hand side of your science notebook. Use what you have learned to create the left-hand page for your notebook.

Mechanical waves travel through matter, causing the particles of that medium (matter) to vibrate. There are two kinds of mechanical waves: transverse waves and longitudinal waves (compression).

- In a **transverse wave**, the particles move in an up-and-down motion. Light waves are an example of transverse waves.
- In a **longitudinal wave**, the motion of the particles is a back-and-forth motion. The parts where the waves are close together are called **compressions**. The parts where the waves are spread out are called **rarefactions**. For example, sound waves are longitudinal waves.

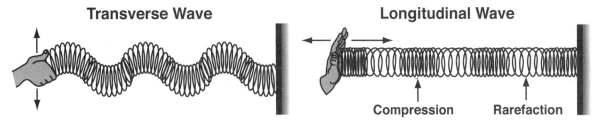

Transverse Wave

Longitudinal Wave

Compression   Rarefaction

How to Create Your Left-Hand Notebook Page

Complete the following steps to create the left-hand page of your physical science notebook. Use lots of color.

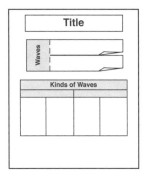

Step 1: Cut out the title and glue it to the top of the notebook page.

Step 2: Cut out the flap chart. Cut on the solid line to create two vocabulary flaps. Apply glue to the back of the gray tab and attach below the title. Write the correct definition under each flap.

Step 3: Cut out the second chart. Apply glue to the back and attach at the bottom of page.

Step 4: Cut apart the picture cards and glue in the correct boxes on the chart.

Demonstrate What You Have Learned

Study the types of waves and their properties using a slinky on a smooth floor. (1) Stretch a slinky out between you and a partner, to a length of about four meters. Move one end of the slinky back and forth on the floor repeatedly, creating a transverse wave. Vary the rate at which your hand moves. (2) Next, create a series of longitudinal waves by moving your hand toward and away from your partner.

Kinds of Waves

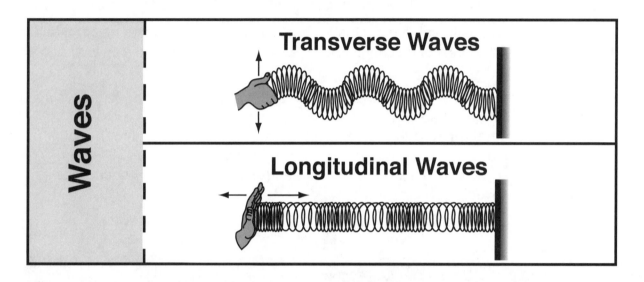

Kinds of Waves

Transverse Wave		Longitudinal Wave	

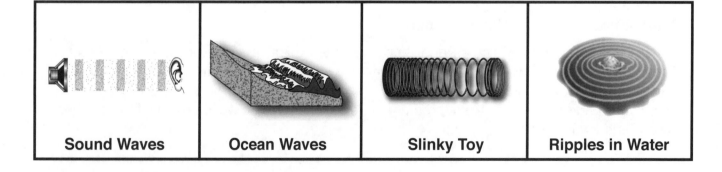

| Sound Waves | Ocean Waves | Slinky Toy | Ripples in Water |

Light

Mini-Lesson

Read the following information. Then cut out and attach this box to the right-hand side of your science notebook. Use what you have learned to create the left-hand page for your notebook.

Light travels in the form of electromagnetic waves. **Light** is a kind of energy produced by the vibrations of electrically charged particles. The energy from the vibrating electrons is partly electric and partly magnetic; that is why this form of energy is referred to as **electromagnetic waves**.

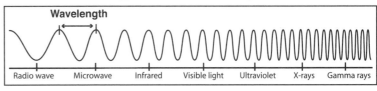

Light waves are classified by frequency into the following types: radio waves, microwaves, infrared, visible light, ultraviolet, X-rays, and gamma rays, which make up the electromagnetic spectrum. The **electromagnetic spectrum** is the complete range of these electromagnetic waves. The only part of the electromagnetic spectrum that can be detected by the human eye is **visible light**. Visible light consists of all the colors of the rainbow: red, orange, yellow, green, blue, indigo, and violet. You can use the acronym **ROY G. BIV** to remember the order of the colors.

Properties of Light

- Light spreads out in all directions from its source.
- Light travels in straight lines called rays.
- Light travels about 186,282 miles per second or 299,792 kilometers per second.
- Light can travel in a vacuum. A vacuum is empty space. Light can travel through empty space as well as matter.

How to Create Your Left-Hand Notebook Page

Complete the following steps to create the left-hand page of your physical science notebook. Use lots of color.

Step 1: Cut out the title and glue it to the top of the notebook page.

Step 2: Color the diagram using the acronym **ROY G. BIV.**
Cut out the diagram box. Apply glue to the back and attach below the title.

Step 3: Cut out the flap chart. Apply glue to the back of the gray tab. Draw the electromagnetic spectrum wavelength on the front. Write the correct definition under the flap.

Demonstrate What You Have Learned

Observe the colors of visible light. Shine a flashlight on a CD in a darkened room. What colors did you see?

Light

Visible Light Diagram

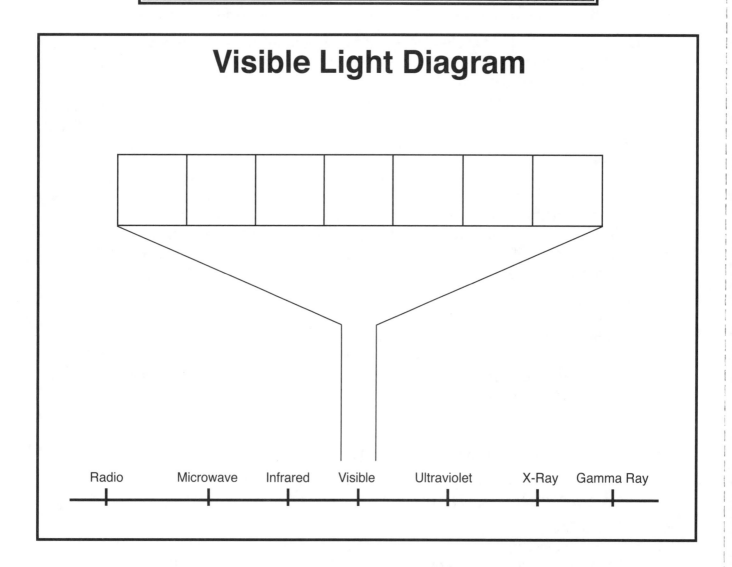

Radio | Microwave | Infrared | Visible | Ultraviolet | X-Ray | Gamma Ray

Electromagnetic Spectrum

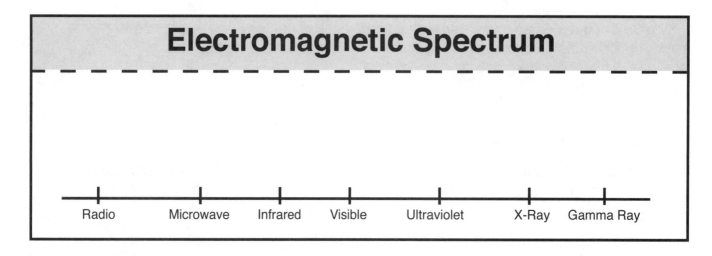

Radio | Microwave | Infrared | Visible | Ultraviolet | X-Ray | Gamma Ray

Light at a Surface

Mini-Lesson

Read the following information. Then cut out and attach this box to the right-hand side of your science notebook. Use what you have learned to create the left-hand page for your notebook.

Three things can happen to light when it hits the surface of an object.

- **Reflection** is the light energy bouncing off an object or surface. When waves reflect off a surface, they obey the **Law of Reflection**. According to this law, light will always be reflected by a surface at the same angle at which it hits the surface. Reflection from a smooth surface is called **specular reflection**; reflection from a rough surface is called **diffuse reflection**.
- **Transmission** is light energy passing through matter. Light passes through some materials more easily than others. Light passes through water, air, and glass easily because they are transparent. You can see through **transparent** matter because light passes through it. Some matter transmits some but not all of the light that hits it; this matter is **translucent**. **Opaque** matter does not transmit any light. Light always travels in a straight line, except when refraction occurs. **Refraction** is light energy bending as it moves from one medium into another medium. An example is when light travels through the Earth's atmosphere, which has lots of thick, moving air in it.
- **Absorption** is when the atoms in matter absorb light; the absorbed light energy is converted into some other form, such as thermal energy. Objects get their color from selective absorption. Grass looks green because it absorbs all the colors of light except green. Green light gets reflected to your eyes. White objects look white because they reflect all colors of light and absorb none. Black objects look black because they absorb all colors of light and reflect none.

How to Create Your Left-Hand Notebook Page

Complete the following steps to create the left-hand page of your physical science notebook. Use lots of color.

Step 1: Cut out the title and glue it to the top of the notebook page.

Step 2: Cut out the flap chart. Apply glue to the back of the gray tab and attach below the title. Write the correct name of the type of reflection illustrated in each picture. Write the definition for the Law of Reflection under the flap.

Step 3: Cut out the chart. Apply glue to the back and attach below the flap chart. Write the correct definition for each word.

Step 4: Cut out the vocabulary flap. Apply glue to the gray tab and attach at the bottom of the page. Write the correct definition under the flap.

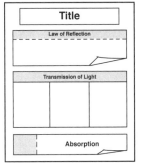

Demonstrate What You Have Learned

Think about what you learned about refraction and then observe the night sky. How does refraction explain why stars appear to twinkle?

Light at a Surface

Law of Reflection

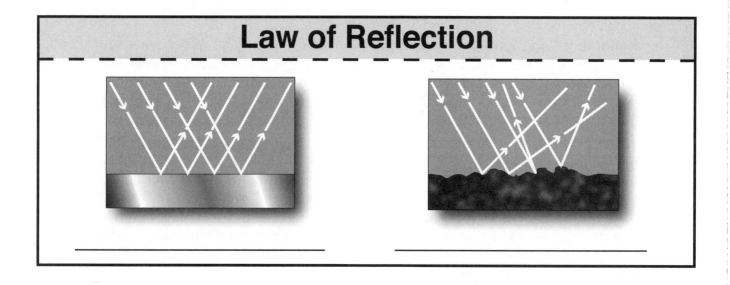

Transmission of Light

Transparent	Translucent	Opaque
Definition: _____	Definition: _____	Definition: _____

Absorption of Light

Sound Properties

Mini-Lesson

Read the following information. Then cut out and attach this box to the right-hand side of your science notebook. Use what you have learned to create the left-hand page for your notebook.

Sound is a mechanical wave that is caused by the back-and-forth vibration of the particles of the medium through which the wave is moving.

Sound Properties

Compression   Rarefaction

Sound waves are longitudinal (compression) waves.

- **Amplitude** is the distance a wave moves (the maximum height of a wave crest or depth of a trough) from its resting position. The larger the amplitude, the more energy carried by the wave.
- **Loudness** (volume) is the intensity of sound. It is measured in **decibels (dB)**. Decibel levels for humans range from 0, the very threshold of human hearing, to 180, a rocket engine.
- **Frequency** is the number of waves produced in a given time. The faster something vibrates, the higher the pitch or frequency.
- **Pitch** is the word used to describe how high or low a sound is that we hear. Pitch is measured in **hertz (Hz)**; one hertz is equal to one wave per second. Example: A tuba vibrates slowly and produces a low pitch. A flute vibrates quickly and produces a high pitch.

How to Create Your Left-Hand Notebook Page

Complete the following steps to create the left-hand page of your physical science notebook. Use lots of color.

Step 1: Cut out the title and glue it to the top of the notebook page.

Step 2: Cut out the diagram box. Draw a sound wave and label the parts.

Step 3: Cut out the flap chart. Cut on the solid lines to create four vocabulary flaps. Apply glue to the back of the gray tab and attach at the bottom of the page.

Step 4: Write the correct definition under each flap.

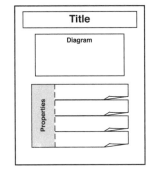

Demonstrate What You Have Learned

Place five empty soda bottles or drinking glasses (glass and the same size) in a line on a table. Fill one bottle with water almost to the top. Fill the second bottle about three-fourths full, the third half full, and leave the last bottle empty. Tap the side of each bottle gently with a wooden spoon. What did you observe about pitch?

Sound Properties

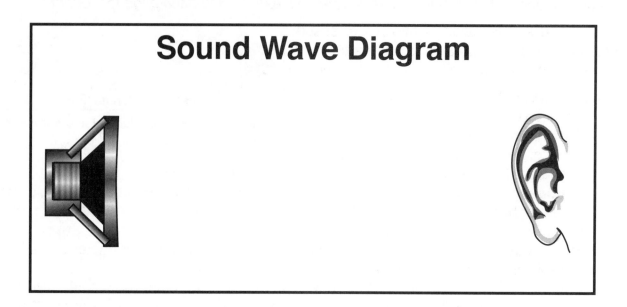

Sound Wave Diagram

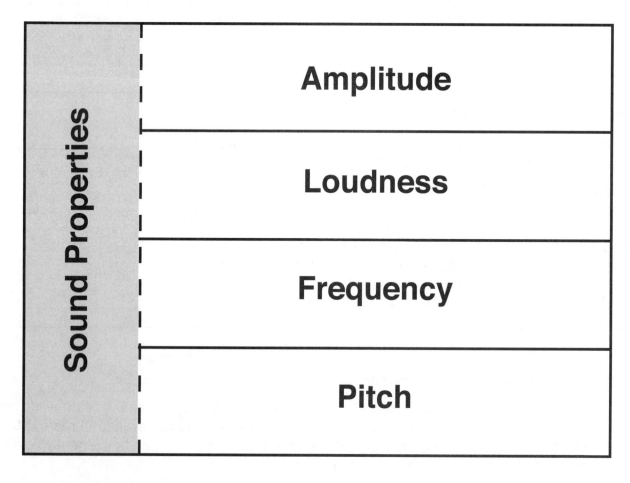

Sound Properties

Amplitude

Loudness

Frequency

Pitch

Electricity

Mini-Lesson

Read the following information. Then cut out and attach this box to the right-hand side of your science notebook. Use what you have learned to create the left-hand page for your notebook.

Electricity is the result of the movement of electrons. The protons and electrons of an atom are attracted to each other. They both carry an **electrical charge**: protons have a positive charge (+), and electrons have a negative charge (-). Like magnets, opposite charges attract each other. When an atom is in balance, it has an equal number of protons and electrons. When atoms are not balanced, they need to gain an electron. Electrons can be made to move from one atom to another. (A proton, which has a

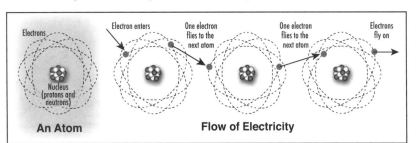

positive charge, attracts an electron, which has a negative charge). When an electron moves between atoms, a current of electricity is created. As one electron is attached to an atom and another electron is lost, it creates a flow of electricity.

Electricity flows easily through some materials, and other materials resist the flow of electricity. **Insulators**, materials such as plastic, rubber, cloth, and glass, hold electrons tightly. **Conductors** are materials that let electrons move more freely. Most metals are good conductors of electricity. Electricity is measured in units called **watts**. One watt is a very small amount of power. A **kilowatt** represents 1,000 watts. A **kilowatt-hour (kWh)** is equal to the energy of 1,000 watts working for one hour. The amount of electricity a power plant generates or a customer uses over a period of time is measured in kilowatt-hours.

How to Create Your Left-Hand Notebook Page

Complete the following steps to create the left-hand page of your physical science notebook. Use lots of color.

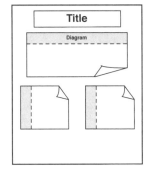

Step 1: Cut out the title and glue it to the top of the notebook page.

Step 2: Cut out the diagram box. Apply glue to the back of the gray tab and attach below the title. Under the flap, write an explanation of how a current of electricity is created.

Step 3: Cut out the two vocabulary flaps. Apply glue to the back of the gray tabs and attach at the bottom of the page.

Step 4: Cut out the four picture cards and glue under the correct vocabulary flaps.

Demonstrate What You Have Learned

Use your home's electric meter to measure how many kilowatt-hours (kWh) of electricity you use in one day. Take a reading at the same time on Day #1 and Day #2; subtract the meter reading on Day #1 from Day #2.

Electricity

How Electricity Flows Diagram

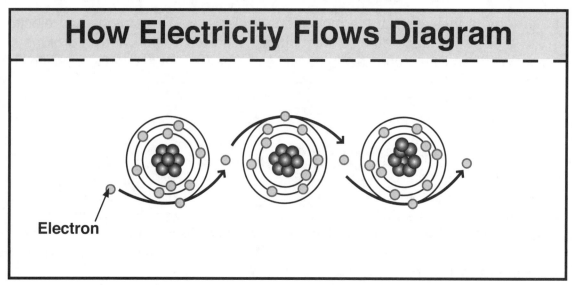

Electron

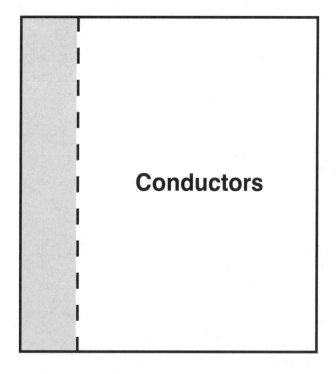

Conductors

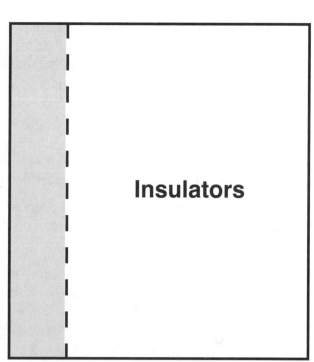

Insulators

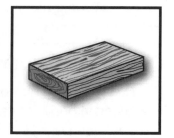

Static Electricity

Read the following information. Then cut out and attach this box to the right-hand side of your science notebook. Use what you have learned to create the left-hand page for your notebook.

Most objects have a neutral charge (no overall charge). They have the same number of protons and electrons.

Static electricity is the build-up of an electrical charge on the surface of an object. It's called "static" because the charges remain in one area for a while instead of moving to another area. A **static charge** is formed when two surfaces (neutral) touch each other, causing the electrons to move from one object to another. For example, rub a dry cloth on a glass rod. The cloth will gain electrons and become negatively charged. The rod loses electrons and becomes positively charged. Remember: items with different charges (positive and negative) will attract, while items with similar charges (positive and positive) will push away from each other—sort of like a magnet. There are three methods by which charges can be transferred to build up static electricity: friction, conduction, and induction.

- **Friction**: Objects can acquire charges (electrons) through the rubbing of one surface against another. For example, rubbing a balloon on a wool sweater and then holding it near your hair. Your hair will be attracted to the balloon.
- **Conduction**: Charges (electrons) may be transferred through direct contact with other objects. For example, walking across a carpet in the winter in your socks. Electrons are transferred from the carpet to the socks. You may see sparks.
- **Induction**: A charge (electrons) may be induced in other objects without contact, with no transfer of electrons. For instance, when you walk across the carpet in stocking feet and reach for the doorknob. You may get zapped before your hand touches the knob.

How to Create Your Left-Hand Notebook Page

Complete the following steps to create the left-hand page of your physical science notebook. Use lots of color.

Step 1: Cut out the title and glue it to the top of the notebook page.
Step 2: Cut out the puzzle flaps. Apply glue to the back of each gray tab and attach below the title. Write the correct definition under each flap.

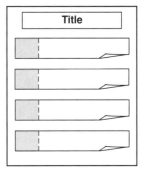

Demonstrate What You Have Learned

Turn the faucet on so that you have a small, 1/8 inch thick stream of water flowing. Now, briskly rub a balloon on a wool sweater. Slowly bring the balloon near the water. Think about what you learned in the Mini-Lesson. What caused the water to bend away from the balloon?

Static Electricity

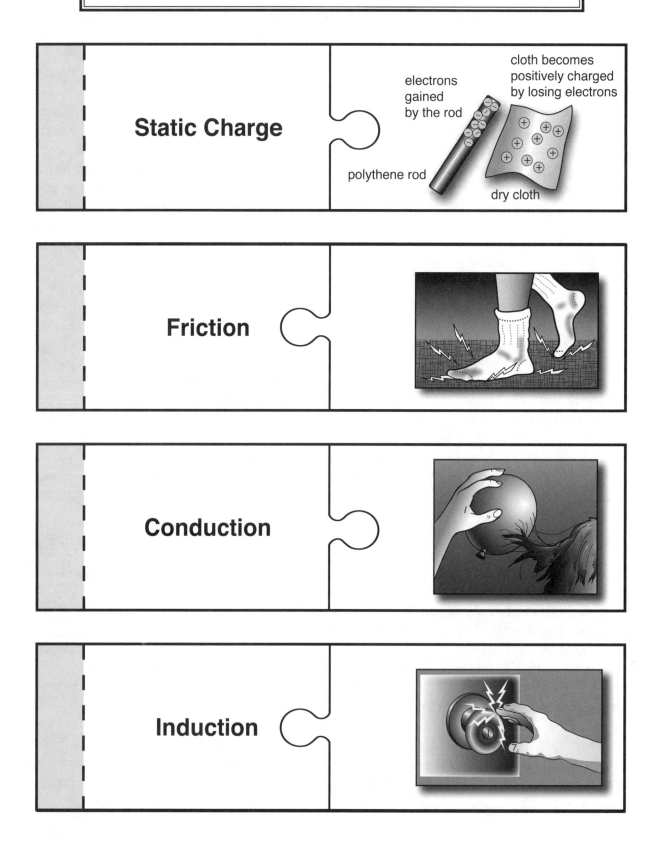

Static Charge

electrons gained by the rod

cloth becomes positively charged by losing electrons

polythene rod

dry cloth

Friction

Conduction

Induction

Current Electricity

Mini-Lesson

Read the following information. Then cut out and attach this box to the right-hand side of your science notebook. Use what you have learned to create the left-hand page for your notebook.

An **electric current** is the flow of electricity through wires. An electrical current must move through an electric circuit. An **electrical circuit** is a continuous path of flowing electrons from a source, through wires and appliances and back to the source. Some materials carry electric current better than others. A **conductor** is a material that will carry (conduct) electric current. An **insulator** is a material that does not conduct electricity.

There are two kinds of current. **Alternating current (AC)** flows in one direction, then the direction reverses, or alternates. The flow of the current changes direction 60 times per second. Electric companies provide homes and businesses with alternating current. **Direct current (DC)** is the flow of electricity in a circuit that moves in only one direction. Flashlight batteries produce direct current.

The SI unit of measurement for the rate of flow of electric current is the **ampere** or **amp (I)**. **Resistance** is a measure of how much a material opposes the flow of electric current through it. The SI unit of measurement for resistance is the **ohm (Ω)**. **Voltage** is the difference in electrical potential energy between two places in a circuit. The SI unit of measurement for voltage is the **volt (V)**.

George Ohm, a physicist, discovered a very important relationship between voltage in volts (V), current in amps (I), and resistance in ohms (R). Electricians use Ohm's Law to determine the efficiency of electrical circuits for safety purposes. The equation, called **Ohm's Law** is **V = I x R**.

How to Create Your Left-Hand Notebook Page

Complete the following steps to create the left-hand page of your physical science notebook. Use lots of color.

Step 1: Cut out the title and glue it to the top of the notebook page.
Step 2: Cut out the flap chart. Cut on the solid lines to create nine vocabulary flaps. Apply glue to the back of the gray tab and attach below the title.
Step 3: Write the correct definition under each flap.

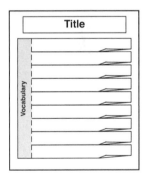

Demonstrate What You Have Learned

Use what you have learned about Ohm's Law to calculate the problem below.

<u>Problem</u>: If you have a current of 1.2 amps flowing through a device with a resistance of

10 ohms, the voltage is _____.

53

Current Electricity

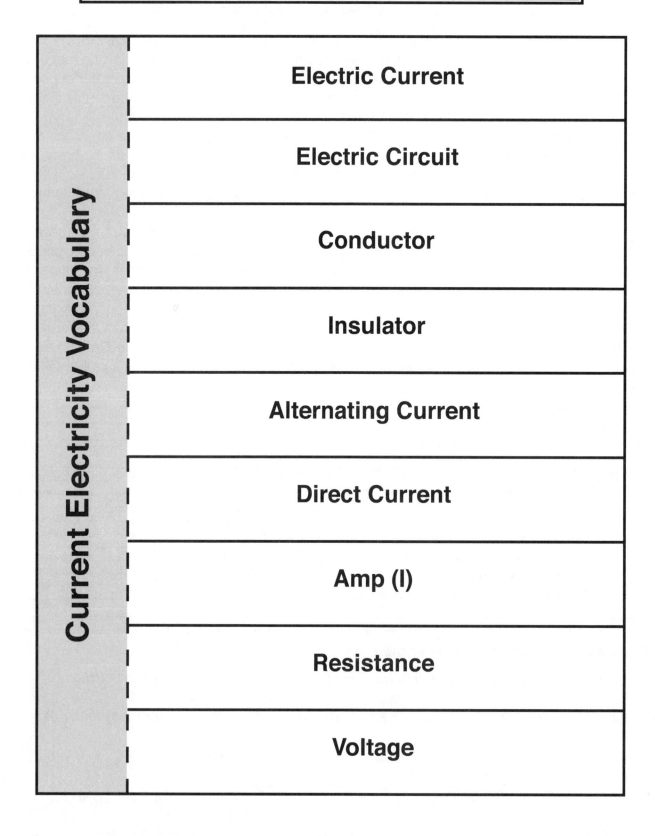

Current Electricity Vocabulary

- Electric Current
- Electric Circuit
- Conductor
- Insulator
- Alternating Current
- Direct Current
- Amp (I)
- Resistance
- Voltage

Parts of an Electric Circuit

Mini-Lesson

Read the following information. Then cut out and attach this box to the right-hand side of your science notebook. Use what you have learned to create the left-hand page for your notebook.

Electrical circuits are used to convert electrical energy into light, sound, and heat energy. An **electrical circuit**, or closed circuit, is a complete path through which electrons flow from an energy source, through a conducting wire and appliance, and back to the energy source. In order for current to flow, the path must have no breaks. An **open circuit (off)** has a break; a **closed circuit (on)** has no breaks. There are four parts to an electrical circuit.

Parts of an Electric Circuit

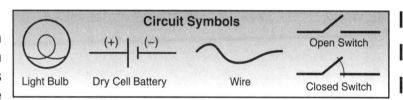

* The **power source** can be either a battery or an electrical outlet in a house. Its job is to provide energy to the electrons, allowing them to move throughout the circuit.
* A **load** is any device that draws power, such as a light bulb.
* **Wires** connect the energy source to the load.
* A **switch** is a device that can open or close the circuit without having to disconnect wires from any component.

How to Create Your Left-Hand Notebook Page

Complete the following steps to create the left-hand page of your physical science notebook. Use lots of color.

Step 1: Cut out the title and glue it to the top of the notebook page.

Step 2: Cut out the first diagram box. Label each part of the diagram. Apply glue to the back of the box and attach below the title.

Step 3: Cut out the second diagram box. Using circuit symbols, draw and label the parts of an open circuit. Apply glue to the back of the box and attach at the bottom of the page.

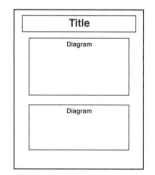

Demonstrate What You Have Learned

Build a simple electric circuit. A circuit includes a power source (battery), a load (light bulb) and a switch connected to each other in series (meaning that wires connect the battery to the switch, the switch to the light bulb and the light bulb back to the other end of the battery).

Parts of an Electric Circuit

Closed Circuit Diagram

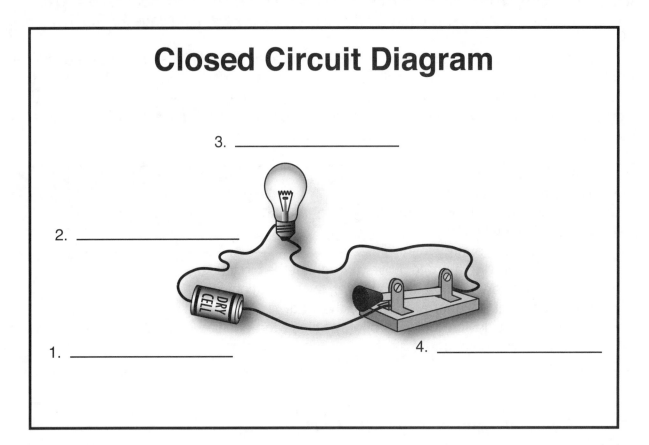

3. _____

2. _____

1. _____

4. _____

Open Circuit Diagram

Types of Circuits

Mini-Lesson

Read the following information. Then cut out and attach this box to the right-hand side of your science notebook. Use what you have learned to create the left-hand page for your notebook.

Electrical circuits are either series or parallel. A **series circuit** has a single path for electric current to flow. For example, older Christmas lights were often wired as a series circuit. If one light burns out, it causes a break in the circuit. There is no path for the current to take, so the other lights go out as well. A **parallel circuit** has more than one path for electric current to flow. Therefore, if one path in a parallel circuit has a break in it, the electrical current can still travel through another path that allows other devices in the circuit to operate. Homes and businesses are wired using parallel circuits.

Series Circuit

Parallel Circuit

How to Create Your Left-Hand Notebook Page

Complete the following steps to create the left-hand page of your physical science notebook. Use lots of color.

Step 1: Cut out the title and glue it to the top of the notebook page.
Step 2: Cut out the diagram boxes. Apply glue to the back of each gray tab and attach to the page.
Step 3: Cut out the picture cards and glue on the front of each flap to create the correct diagram. Draw lines between the picture cards to show how a wire connects each item to complete the circuit.
Step 4: Write the correct definition under each flap.

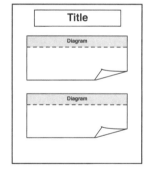

Demonstrate What You Have Learned

Using flashlight bulbs, several insulated wires, and D-cell batteries, create a series and a parallel circuit. Each circuit should have two or more bulbs. Connect all wires and observe the light bulbs. Now unscrew one bulb in each circuit. Observe the remaining bulbs. What happened? Why did it happen?

Types of Circuits

Series Circuit Diagram

Parallel Circuit Diagram

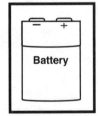
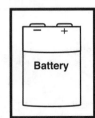

Magnetism

Mini-Lesson

Read the following information. Then cut out and attach this box to the right-hand side of your science notebook. Use what you have learned to create the left-hand page for your notebook.

A **magnet** is a device that attracts certain metals, such as iron, nickel, and cobalt. Magnets come in a variety of sizes, shapes, and strengths. One of the most common magnets is a bar magnet. Another is the horseshoe magnet. No matter what the shape, the magnet will have two **poles**, or ends. One pole is a north pole; and the other is a south pole. **Magnetic force** is the attractive or repulsive force between the poles of magnets. If two magnets are placed near each other, the north pole of one will **attract** (move closer together) the south pole of the other. If you place north poles toward each other, they will **repel** (move apart) each other. If you place south poles toward each other, they will repel each other. Remember: like poles repel and unlike poles attract each other.

A **magnetic field** is the space around a magnet where there is a magnetic force. This invisible force exists around every magnet and can be observed by using iron filings. When iron filings are scattered around a magnet, they always take the same shape. The curved lines of iron filings show the magnetic field around the magnet.

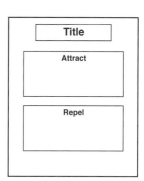

How to Create Your Left-Hand Notebook Page

Complete the following steps to create the left-hand page of your physical science notebook. Use lots of color.

Step 1: Cut out the title and glue it to the top of the notebook page.

Step 2: Cut out the two boxes. Apply glue to the back and attach below the title.

Step 3: Cut out the picture cards. Apply glue to the back and place in the correct box.

Title
Attract
Repel

Demonstrate What You Have Learned

Place a bar magnet in a plastic sandwich bag and lay it on a table. Place a sheet of white paper on top of the bag. Sprinkle iron filings over the paper. The filings form a pattern that represents the magnetic field of the magnet. Draw a diagram of the pattern on the left-hand page of your notebook.

Magnetism

Attract

Repel

N		S		S		N

S		N		S		N

S		N		N		S

N		S		N		S

Electromagnetism

Mini-Lesson

Read the following information. Then cut out and attach this box to the right-hand side of your science notebook. Use what you have learned to create the left-hand page for your notebook.

Electromagnetism is magnetism resulting from electric charge in motion. Electricity and magnetism are closely related. The movement of electrons causes both. **Electricity** comes from the flow of electrons from one atom to another. **Magnetism** is the alignment of electrons in the atom in the same direction, creating a magnetic field.

 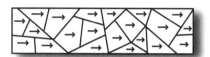

An **electromagnet** is a type of magnet in which the magnetic field is produced by an electric current. Every electric current has its own magnetic field. This magnetic force can be used to make an electromagnet. Wrapping an insulated wire around a nail and then attaching the ends of the wire to a battery is a way to create a temporary magnet called an electromagnet. The advantage of an electromagnet over a permanent magnet is that it can be turned on and off, and the strength of the magnetism can be varied. The strength of an electromagnet depends on two main things: the size of the electric current you use and the number of times you coil the wire. Increase either or both of these, and you get a more powerful electromagnet.

Wire coiled around iron nail

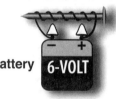

Battery 6-VOLT

How to Create Your Left-Hand Notebook Page

Complete the following steps to create the left-hand page of your physical science notebook. Use lots of color.

Step 1: Cut out the title and glue it to the top of the notebook page.
Step 2: Cut out the flap chart. Cut on the solid line to create two flaps. Apply glue to the back of the gray tab and attach below the title.
Step 3: Cut out the two picture cards and place under the correct flap.
Step 4: Cut out the diagram box. Apply glue to the back of the gray tab and attach at the bottom of the page. Draw a diagram of an electromagnet on the front. Write the correct definition under the flap.

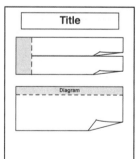

Demonstrate What You Have Learned

Construct an electromagnet. Using a piece of insulated bell wire one meter long, start about 40 centimeters from one end; wrap the wire tightly around an iron nail 20 times. Connect the ends of the wire to a 1.5-volt battery. Try picking up paper clips with the nail.

Electromagnetism

Electron Flow in Electricity

Electron Flow in Magnetism

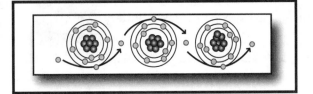   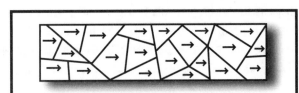

Electromagnet Diagram